©2016 ILUMINA PRODUCCIONES, S.A. De C.V.
All rights reserved.

ISBN: 978-1-943488-02-5

No part of this publication may be reproduced, distributed, or transmitted in any form or by any means, including photocopying, recording, or other electronic or mechanical methods, without the prior written permission of the copyright holder. The infringement of such rights may constitute an offense against intellectual property.

Published by: Editorial ILUMINA S.A. de C.V.

Printed in Mexico
By Offset Santiago S.A. de C.V.
Río San Joaquín 436, Col. Ampliación Granada
CP 11520, México D.F.

Silent Silus in: Lucky me!
First edition: June 2016

Layout and editorial design: Paola Alonso.
Conceptual Art: Rosa Maria Campos Cruz.
Editorial review: Shaula Vega. Jonathan Venguer.
Hector Fernandez.

Silent Silus in:
LUCKY ME!

Text and illustrations by BIBIANA DOMIT

Hi, my name is Silus.
I am a great athlete! I love to play all types of sports. My favorite one is soccer.

I am a very fast runner, but when it comes to talking I am more of a quiet type, which is why my friends
call me "Silent Silus".

My friends also say I am very lucky,
because in sports I always win.
Speaking about luck, let me tell you about the day
I understood what luck really is.

It was Sunday. I woke up before sunrise.
I was very excited because
I had a big tournament that day.

I got ready and ran to the soccer field
while it was still dark.
I practiced passes, dribbles and shots on goal.

My LUCKY CLEATS!
The cleats I used for my big tournaments.
The ones that always helped me win.

The moment arrived and I entered the field with my team. As I stood there, I noticed something terrible. One of my lucky cleats was torn!

Although I didn't want to, I had to obey my coach.
As I took them off,
I quietly said to myself:
"Without my lucky cleats, I will never win."

As the game began, I tried running, kicking and shooting goals. But I was playing awfully bad. The first half of the game ended and the other team was wining 2-0.

During half time at the locker room,
our coach was giving out strategies and plays.
I couldn't even look at the board.
I felt sad and worried.

Suddenly, an image came to mind. It was my granny!

I remember she used to say: "Luck is not on things, it is in the heart and mind of those who set a goal and practice everyday to realize it."

I didn't really know what she meant,
but at that moment I needed anything that could
help me win the game and save my team!

I decided to give it a try. I closed my eyes
and listened to the fast beat of my heart.
Then, I silently whispered: "Heart, can you
give me luck? I really need it now."

But my heart didn't answer.

Maybe it was because
I forgot to say please.
Or I didn't speak loud enough?
I tried again. This time
I shouted with all my might:
"Heart, you have to help me!
Give me luck, PLEASE!!!"

But again I heard nothing.
Just silence.
My heart didn't reply.

"Maybe my heart doesn't know
what luck means".
So I explained what luck is
and what it feels like.

"Luck gives you confidence and strength.
With luck you feel invincible!
When luck is with you, you're not afraid
of anything because you know you can
achieve everything you want!"

As I spoke about luck,
I remembered the dedication I had put
into my soccer training every day.
The moments I felt really tired
but kept going on.
I remember I always gave my best.

Thinking about this made me feel very confident and strong!

I went out to the field to catch up with my team, and I ran and played like a champion!

Within minutes I scored one, two and three goals!

The game was over, and my team won!
But you know who won the most?
I did! Because I learned something very special.

I learned that luck is not on things,
but inside all of us.
In our dedication, daily practice and constant effort
to achieve our goals!

Trust yourself!
Commit to your dreams,
and remember the more you practice
the luckier you'll get.

TULLYS

Silent Silus

Silus is a very active boy who loves playing
outdoors. His favorite sport is soccer.
He is the fastest runner and always
wins the gold medals!
A quiet but strong athlete with a big heart,
that knows real champions
are built with practice every day.

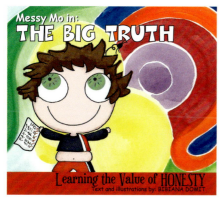
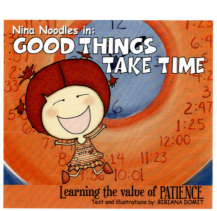
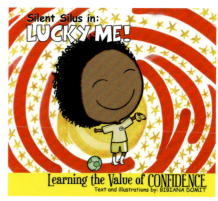
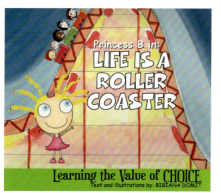
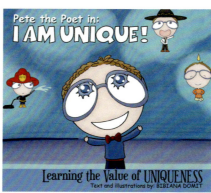
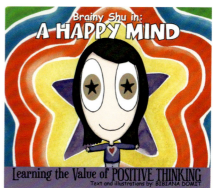

www.tullys.tv